Behind Door #3:

Choose With Your Eyes Wide Open

To the free little library
Please choose
your options
carefully —

Jacki
Gethner

Jacki Gethner

with Jen Violi

Behind Door #3:
Choose With Your Eyes Wide Open

Copyright @ 2013

Behind Door #3 may be purchased through book dealers and on line book stores, at www.SacredLife.com, and Jacki Gethner's website: jackigethner.com.

ISBN: 978-09728592-6-4
ISBN: 0972859268
Library of Congress Control Number: 2013943829

The information, ideas, and suggestions in this book are not intended as a substitute for professional advice. Before following any suggestions contained in this book, consult your physician or mental health professional. Neither the authors nor the publisher shall be liable or responsible for any loss or damage allegedly arising as a consequence of your use or application of any information or suggestions in this book.

Cover Design by: Miko Radcliffe - miko@drawingacrowd.net

Sacred Life Publishers™
www.SacredLife.com
Printed in the United States of America

Dedication

In Memory of My Friend

Bonnie

Acknowledgements

This book is driven by the desire to help women navigating this new world of dating and friendships to find happiness while staying healthy and safe.

I would like to first thank the thousands of women who have shared stories with me of their personal journeys.

I thank Jen Violi, my writer, for her incredible use of words that took the visions I had for this book and made them real and for understanding my dedication to sharing this information. She is the author of *Putting Makeup on Dead People.* As a developmental editor and writing coach, she wrangles manuscripts and mentors writers as they discover the books they're meant to write. Jen lives in Portland, Oregon. www.jenvioli.com.

I am forever grateful to Michael Linder who patiently put up with me as we continued to play with words, placement, and punctuation.

I acknowledge with respect Jack Cox, WOACA board member, for his support and listening ear whenever frustrations arose.

To Sharon Lund, I give thanks for her gift of publishing this book and knowing why these topics need to be spoken aloud among women openly and honestly.

Lastly, I want to express gratitude to Kim Breas for supporting this venture and reminding me that my cause - while not easy for many to face - is imperative to be continued as we move through our lives.

In the words of Daisaku Ikeda: *"A great human revolution in just a single individual will help achieve a change in the destiny of a nation and, further, will enable a change in the destiny of all humankind"*.

Contents

Full Disclosure

This book is not intended to give you answers, but rather to remind you that you have a choice.

When I was about ten, I looked forward to the game show *Let's Make a Deal.* I loved the fun and adventure of watching people make choices, take risks, consider the value of what they had and then decide if they wanted to trade it in for something else. I anticipated the possibilities behind those three doors.

The choices I would have made back then are not the choices I would make now. For women over fifty, life is different. We know more. When you get to be our age, you've got a steamer trunk full of baggage and some hard-learned lessons.

At the same time, in some ways, we know less. We have new things to learn. Regardless, we have the power to choose.

As I worked on this book, considering the risks we women take, what we'll give up to get something else, and the opportunities we have to make exciting choices, I couldn't help but think of *Let's Make a Deal.* And I started to think of those three doors in a new way, representing different paths we might take:

1

Door #1: keep making the same kinds of choices based on what we knew way back when;

Door #2: look to friends or role models or celebrities and copy their choices;

OR (and this is the one I'm rooting for)

Door #3: gather all of that information (who we were, what we knew, what others do), look at it with our eyes open and our minds and hearts engaged, and make the choice that is best for the particularities of us in the present moment.

Sometimes our choices will lead to joyful connection and sometimes to a memory of an unsatisfied relationship. The bottom line is that we have to be our own best judges. I hope after reading this book, you'll choose Door #3.

We might like to believe that all intimate relationships fit the perceived ideal of our parents or grandparents who stayed partnered with just one person for fifty or sixty years.

However, divorce happens, heartbreak happens, and death can separate us from someone we love after just a few short years. We can find ourselves dating for the first time in decades, applying "the rules" from the way we did it back then to what turns out to be a whole different game now.

"More than 60% of individuals over 60 have sex at least once a month, and yet they are rarely considered to be "at risk" for an STD (sexual transmitted disease). Even those who are no longer sexually active may still have a sexually transmitted infection for which they were never treated or screened, and the long term neurological side effects of diseases such as HIV and syphilis may be easily be mistaken for other diseases of aging."[1]

"Individuals who are infected with STDs are at least two to five times more likely than uninfected individuals to acquire HIV infection if they are exposed to the virus through sexual contact."

(Wasserheit, 1992)

"Semen can stay in the vagina for days after sex, while men are only exposed to HIV infected fluids during sex. Semen left in the vagina means a longer exposure to the virus for women."

(US Dept of Health and Human Services)

Beyond HIV, hepatitis is the most common blood borne viral infection in the U.S. and the most chronic cause of liver disease in the US (accounting for 40 - 60% of

---

[1] "Age is Not a Condom: Old Sex Does Not Mean Safe Sex" Feb. 8, 2012
About.com Guide, Elizabeth Boskey, PhD.

all cases), and one in thirty-three baby boomers are unaware that they have the virus until they have advanced liver damage. (Please be tested—resources for you are on page 127).

So where does all of this leave us? Well, I think it leaves us with more information, which means more power to make well-informed choices. It could be easy to feel overwhelmed or even powerless, but this isn't about losing power. This is about gaining the power that comes with knowledge and awareness. Behind Door #3 is your strength, your wisdom, and a chance to live as the whole, beautiful woman you are.

Behind Door #3 Is *You*

I wrote this book as a way to help women over fifty identify how they might make decisions in various situations of intimate involvement with another person.

As you read the following scenarios, let yourself enter the minds and hearts of these characters. Take some time to answer the questions about similar situations that you might have experienced. Note what lessons you learned.

You might not be a widow, or bi-sexual, or in recovery from an addiction, but you do know what it's like to be at a crossroads, to make a choice that turns out badly, and to wish you'd known about or considered other options.

You might have gotten used to letting others decide for you, but it's time for you to take the reins again. That's why you picked up this book. You're ready.

I gained a whole new understanding of choice when I was a high school junior. Oak Park River Forest High School allowed us to choose our own curriculum. Until then, I had struggled as a student and felt stuck.

But my science teacher, a skinny man with a big heart, said, "Jacki, this is your chance to learn outside the book." That year, I went from C's and D's to A's and B's, because I was given options. Some of my choices worked out, and some didn't. The bottom line was that I got to validate what worked for me, not just by reading it out of a book.

Since that time, I've worked hard to accept my failings as well as my victories. When I make a mistake, I've learned to say, "Oh well," followed not too long after by a hopeful and determined, "Okay, what's next?"

Consider using this book as a guide to who you want to be from this day forth, as support while you look for your next relationship. Don't over-think the process. Be kind to yourself. Learn to say, "Oh well," and "What's next?" The skills we learned before are no longer the skills we can use today.

You've made mistakes, you've moved on, you've lived or struggled or learned from the consequences. That's life. What you write here stays here unless you decide to share it with someone else. My hope is that you'll use this book as an ongoing reference to review lessons learned while you create new experiences.

In real life, some decisions can cost you your life. So use this book to be risky in your mind without jeopardizing your health or your future.

> *"Part of the game now is that women over fifty are in the fastest growth bracket of new HIV cases, and that the heterosexual transmission rate among women over fifty has doubled over the past ten years in the United States."*
>
> **The Centers for Disease Control (CDC)**

Also, know that you don't have to decide everything or change everything right this minute. Small changes and choices can lead to powerful transformations. So crack open Door #3, and see what happens.

That said, here's your first choice:

1. If you want to step into the world of seventy-two year old Sharon, on her first cruise after the death of her husband of fifty years, and finding herself in the midst of a romantic entanglement at sea, turn to page 17.

2. To learn more about why I care so much about these issues, how this book came to be, and why I can be a real buzzkill in an elevator, turn to page 9.

How I Got Here . . .

I can be a real buzz-kill in an elevator.

If I land in one of those metal boxes with a group of women, as the doors close, I turn around and say, "Great, I'm so glad were all gathered here." I look them all in the eye. "Now I've got some important stuff to share about your health."

During twenty-six plus years as a body worker, I've learned when to be gentle and subtle, and when to be direct and assertive. With some particular women's health issues, I've come to understand that there's no time to waste. This is not a conversation to dance around or to have tomorrow. For me, this conversation about women's health is not a luxury, and it's not small talk. It's essential. It's big time.

Let me tell you a story, one of many I could share, to show why I care so deeply about your health and mine.

In 1969 I met Bonnie, who became one of my dearest friends. We traveled many roads together, supporting each other through the challenges of being in bi-racial relationships in the 70's, and in Bonnie's case, of addiction.

By 1976, I'd moved to Boulder, Colorado, and Bonnie was living in Winthrop, Massachusetts. Bonnie's family reached out to me, worried that she had liver cancer, based on both her addiction history and what she'd been saying to them. They asked if I'd be willing to travel at their expense to Winthrop and assess the situation.

Ready to help my good friend, I delayed a job interview, found care for my five year-old son, and hopped on the next available plane to Winthrop.

As always, Bonnie and I were thrilled to see each other, but I could also see that she had been using drugs consistently for a while. On top of that, I learned that she had been involved in several vehicular accidents (luckily, just involving her own car).

On the second day of my visit, a friend of hers came by, was briefly introduced to me, and left shortly after. The encounter felt strange to me. I sensed something was up.

A bit later, I couldn't find Bonnie until I noticed the bathroom was occupied. I knocked on the door.

Bonnie said, "Just a minute, just a minute." She sounded nervous, and I knew why.

I opened the door and found Bonnie sitting on the closed lid of the toilet, injecting drugs.

I became incredibly upset and we had a one sided argument, since as we spoke I could see the Dilaudid was doing its job. She was checked out.

I told Bonnie what I'd given up to be there, about her parents' concern (which was enough to have paid for my trip), and ultimately, that I didn't want to talk to her at all until she was six months clean and sober.

> *"The number of Americans infected with the hepatitis C virus is three to five times the number infected with HIV."*
>
> *"An estimated 5 million American's have already been infected with the hepatitis C virus."*
>
> **Caring Ambassador Program**
> **HepCChallenge.org**

Angered and saddened, I took a cab in the pouring rain back to Logan Airport.

Six months to the day later, Bonnie called to tell me she had gone into treatment the day after I'd left and had been clean for six months.

Beyond that, she was pursuing a position working with other addicts like herself.

I was so glad to hear all of it, until she shared her last bit of news: she'd been diagnosed with HIV. At that point in the epidemic, one very seldom, if at all, heard about women being infected, and my heart was broken for my friend who had become part of a statistic that was just starting to grow.

In 1986, I was attending massage school in Boulder, Colorado, and heard about a conference called AIDS Medicine and Miracles, organized by the Boulder-based organization of the same name, and unique in that it was the first holistic/western medicine AIDS conference to be held in the United States. At that time, those with an HIV diagnosis were usually not only shunned by family and friends, but also had to deal with their medical providers gowning up (including face masks and gloves) for just an office visit. This conference was a much-needed breath of fresh air.

At the conference, I asked one of my sister students to join me in offering chair massage to the conference participants so that we could learn more about this disease and share caring touch with many people, some of whom who hadn't been touched since their diagnosis.

That offering became a launching pad for much more learning and work and many more stories, probably enough for another book. Since that time, I've worked with hundreds of thousands of people either infected or affected by HIV.

In the following years, when I saw Bonnie clean and sober, the joy of our friendship was alive. But the last two times I went to Winthrop - once at the plea of her boyfriend then husband after she'd totaled two cars - her addiction had returned full force. Bonnie was so deep in her addiction that she was shooting up anything she could find.

In July of 1995, when Bonnie's body gave in to complications of AIDS and she died, I couldn't bring myself to make another trip to say goodbye.

In 2009, I was nominated to receive Kaiser Permanente's National Diversity Award for my work in HIV and was chosen as the sole individual recipient. The award included $10,000, which I was free to use in any way I desired.

In tribute to Bonnie's struggle and to support other women and other best friends, I used this money to start my program, *Women of a Certain Age,* all sales from this book will go directly toward my program.

I wanted women to understand the risks, not only in addiction, but also in sexual activity. I wanted to share preventative tools. I wanted to offer a resource for lonely and isolated women, who unknowingly made risky choices so they wouldn't have to be alone.

My program exists not just to encourage women to be safer in intimate situations, but also to create and recreate our female friendships, so that we can have long lifetimes of fun with each other.

The four different experiences of women in this book are just a few of many possibilities. Whether the situations feel realistic to you or not, I encourage you to recognize the common hopes, fears, and worries within and to use these stories as a catalyst for your own reflection and a way to explore your own choices. For a moment, put yourself in the places of these women and see what decisions you might make. Or, if these situations are familiar, consider what choices you might make if you had a do-over.

As you do this, you'll likely notice other feelings surface regarding how you feel about yourself, what you're willing to do for someone else you might (or might not) know very well, and whether or not you're able to make the best decision with the information you already have. I've made sure to include questions and plenty of space to support you in this inevitable and necessary reflection. This is definitely a book you can write in!

At the end of this book is a list of resources for you, not just to inform you about STDs, HIV/AIDS, and hepatitis C but also to educate you to be proactive about your health and well-being. I'm hoping you'll take the time to explore them.

We as women often have this dangerous perception that "it won't happen to me," only motivated to pay attention when someone famous comes forward and claims a disease or condition. Regardless of who comes forward, it *can* be you.

It feels easier to wait until a consequence has happened and then look for a quick fix. But it's so much healthier to be equipped to make informed and grounded choices in the first place. Even if we don't get our needs met, the results of making good decisions for ourselves are worth waiting for.

This isn't about living with fear. It's about living with wisdom and awareness. It is vital that we use this awareness and wisdom in our own lives. When we see our female friends engaging in risky business, it is vital that we share our concerns and offer support

As you turn the next corner in your own relationship odyssey and approach Door #3, take your time. Take a breath. Make one good choice at a time, and trust that those good choices will add up to something wonderful.

To learn more about Jacki, and her program, please visit her website www.jackigethner.com.

Cruisin': Sharon's Story

When Arthur died, Sharon felt like her life might be over, too.

For fifty-two years, they shared life - raised their kids, retired, and then started taking their RV out on the road to travel and visit the grandkids. Sharon had friends, but didn't see them very much. Her relationship with Arthur was at the heart of her life.

When Arthur died, Sharon's friends did all the "right" things. They called to check on her, brought food after the service, and even offered to help clean out Arthur's possessions.

Even with support, Sharon withdrew and kept to herself, not answering or returning phone calls, wondering what on earth a seventy-two year old woman was supposed to do with a big RV and an empty house.

Almost a year after Arthur's death, Sharon's friends thought she might enjoy the cruise they were taking in December. Lucy called Sharon, and in a forgetful moment, Sharon answered the phone.

Lucy invited her on the cruise. "It'll be good for you," she said. "You need to get out and have some fun."

"I don't think so," Sharon said.

"More importantly, it'll be good for all of us. We miss you. It's been a long time," Lucy said.

At this, Sharon paused. It was easier to think about doing something for them. It was also nice to feel missed. Sharon decided Lucy might be right. Maybe she could use the boost of something different and fun.

As the trip approached, Sharon spent more time with her friends, even going out and buying her first new bathing suit in forty years. She'd been an avid swimmer, but since Arthur had been afraid of the water, she'd let that part of her life go. It felt good to rediscover a piece of herself.

As soon as they boarded the ship, Sharon and her friends found an abundance of opportunities to mingle and meet other passengers.

Missing Arthur, Sharon cringed at the couples. Plus, she noticed that the married women looked at her with some suspicion, holding their husbands' hands tighter as Sharon and Lucy walked by. Feeling like a threat - this was new.

During the first few evenings of card games and dances, Sharon had noticed one single man in particular and was surprised to feel a little flutter when she wondered about getting to know him better. This was new, too.

On the third night of the cruise, the man approached Sharon at dinner and introduced himself as Monty. He asked if they could be partners at cards later.

1. If Sharon felt scared that she was betraying Arthur's memory, turn to page 21.

2. If Sharon felt comfortable accepting Monty's invitation to play cards, go to page 25.

3. If neither of these fit for you, share why here:

_____

_____

_____

Now step outside of that thinking and pick one.

Option 1:

Sharon fought the urge to shout, "I'm a married woman." What would Arthur think?

Of course Arthur was dead, but it was hard not to feel like playing cards with another man would be cheating.

Monty's smile was kind and Sharon found herself attracted to him. But the thought that she'd be betraying Arthur was stronger than any attraction she might feel.

"No, thank you," she said to Monty.

As Monty walked away, Lucy said, "It's not too late to change your mind."

"I don't want to talk about it," Sharon said.

And she didn't. For the rest of the cruise, Sharon stayed close to her friends, and went to bed early every night, especially when there were dances in the ballroom.

Each night, before she went to sleep, Sharon told Arthur she loved him and would stay true to his memory. She'd wait and listen, thinking he might somehow whisper, "Thank you."

On the last day of the cruise, Sharon watched Monty walk off the ship with another woman. Sharon imagined for a second that it could have been her, but quickly told herself that was a foolish thought, a young girl's thought, and she was a woman who knew better.

1. How did reading this decision of Sharon's relate or not to your own experiences?

_____

_____

_____

2. What happened to move you past this part of your grief?

_____

_____

_____

3. Did you notice yourself falling back into any other unhealthy patterns as you were grieving?

_____

_____

_____

4. Were you able to ask for help?

_____

_____

_____

5. Have the issues been resolved?

_____

_____

_____

Option 2:

Sharon found playing cards with Monty easier than she expected. It turned out they lived within twenty-five miles of each other and that he'd graduated from the all-boys high school she'd been to once for a dance. She wondered if they'd been in the same room all those years ago.

Monty was kind and fun, and even complimented her dress. While she knew Arthur loved her, he had never been big on the compliments, and Sharon found she enjoyed receiving one.

The next day was a port visit. Monty invited Sharon to spend the day with him walking around the island town. Knowing that her girlfriends would be close, Sharon agreed, with the request that they all meet up for a group lunch.

The morning was fabulous, and at lunch Sharon was a little embarrassed about Monty's gushing about what a great time they had shopping and walking in the sunshine.

That evening, Sharon went with her friends to hear the band playing in the ship ballroom. Monty was there when they arrived and seemed very glad to see her. When Monty gently asked her to join him on the dance floor, Sharon found herself dancing for the first time in over fifty years. The last time she and Arthur had danced was on a date before they were married.

Monty was an excellent dancer. He knew how to lead without making her feel clumsy. As the song continued, she felt Monty pull her closer. To her surprise, she melted into his touch.

After the dance, Monty asked her if they could go for a walk on the deck. Over two hours and a few glasses of wine, they shared stories about their lives.

It turned out Monty had been a widower for three years. His wife had had Parkinson's and for the last few years of her life, he'd been her sole care provider. Sharon was impressed by his commitment to and love for his wife.

Sharon easily described happy times with Arthur, but when she came to the words "heart attack," she couldn't hold back the tears. She stopped speaking.

Monty offered her his handkerchief and put his arm round her, which made her cry even more as she realized she hadn't been touched since Arthur's funeral.

Monty suggested a walk on the deck, and they found their way back to conversation. When he brought her back to her room, he kissed her forehead and said goodnight.

The next day when Sharon saw Monty in the dining room, she felt butterflies in her stomach. He approached her and asked if they could have breakfast together. Her girlfriends hadn't arrived yet, so she agreed, thinking they would join her eventually.

They never showed up, but again she had a wonderful time with Monty and agreed to go on another day trip with him.

Off the ship, Monty looked out for her, and took her hand as a way of expressing companionship. They laughed and enjoyed the sights together, pointing out lovely views or funny items to each other. At one point, Monty leaned over and kissed her.

Sharon felt a thrill she hadn't experienced in a very long time.

Two nights later, after a delicious dinner, a few glasses of wine, and dancing for what seemed like days, they found themselves out on the deck kissing more passionately than they had before.

Monty suggested that maybe they could go to his cabin so as not to be in the public eye.

1. If Sharon agrees to go, despite her nervousness, turn to page 29 2A.

2. If Sharon hesitates and decides to go back inside and have more wine, turn to page 33 2B.

Option 2A:

As soon as Monty closed the door behind them, Sharon felt her neck and shoulders getting tight. She noticed Monty's open suitcase, his socks from yesterday on the floor in the corner.

His unmade bed looked dangerous to her. She felt unmade herself.

Monty pulled her close and whispered in her ear, "I'm so glad you're here." Then he pulled back a bit and leaned in for a kiss.

The kiss felt good, exciting even, but something didn't feel right to Sharon.

She felt the urge to run, but took a deep breath and pushed it down. She was the one who'd agreed to come to Monty's room, after all, so she should be the one to follow through. Not wanting to disappoint Monty or to look foolish, she ignored her instincts, and began to kiss him harder.

At first, Monty responded to this, holding her tighter, but then Sharon felt his grip loosen. He pulled back.

"What is it?" she asked.

"I'm so sorry," Monty said. "I thought I was ready, but I'm not."

"Oh, thank God," Sharon said, relief flooding through the tightness in her neck.

"What?"

"I'm not ready either," she said and they both found their tension dissolving into laughter.

They agreed to take things slow for the rest of the trip, and continued to enjoy each other's company. On the last day of the cruise, they exchanged phone numbers and made a date for coffee the following week.

As Sharon picked up her suitcase on the dock, she realized Lucy had been right. She did feel better, lighter, and she definitely had something to look forward to.

1. Has your own experience allowed you a similar "ending" as Sharon's?

_____

_____

_____

2. If not, what did you learn for "the next time"?

_____

_____

_____

Option 2B:

Although this evening had been lovely, the thought of going back to Monty's cabin filled Sharon with anxiety. The butterflies in her stomach started flying a little too quickly. She looked down at the ground, not sure what to say.

"What do you think?" Monty asked.

Sharon's heart was beating so loudly in her ears that it was hard to think. She just wanted to calm down, but didn't know how. "Maybe we should have another glass of wine and think about it."

Monty agreed and they returned to the ballroom. One more glass of wine turned to two, and they were both tipsy when Sharon said, "Let's go to your cabin."

Monty said, "My thoughts exactly."

Sharon noticed he was slurring his words, but chose to ignore that. The wine made her feel warm and confident.

Back in Monty's room, they kissed and things happened fast. Sharon wasn't quite sure how they landed in Monty's bed, with him on top of her.

It had been so long since she'd been with anyone else - there was only that one man before Arthur - she wasn't sure for a moment what to do. Through the haze of wine and the excitement she was feeling, Sharon managed to get out a one-word question, "Condom?"

"We're over sixty, Sharon," Monty said. "I don't think you're going to get pregnant." He laughed.

His laughter sounded condescending, and any excitement Sharon had been feeling swirled right down the drain. She pushed Monty off of her and sat up.

"I think maybe this was too fast," Sharon said, smoothing out her skirt. "I should go."

1. If Monty lets Sharon walk back to her cabin alone, turn to page 35 2B1.

2. If Monty walks Sharon back to her cabin, turn to page 37 2B2.

Option 2B1:

"You probably should go," Monty said.

Monty sat on the bed and didn't say a word while Sharon buttoned up her blouse and put on her sweater and shoes. The room felt empty, and when she shut the door behind her, it made a hollow sound that echoed in the corridor.

Embarrassed, Sharon avoided Monty the rest of the cruise and withdrew from her friends as well.

When Lucy asked her if she wanted to talk about it, Sharon said no.

On the last day of the cruise, Monty handed her a note with his phone number. Sharon was the one who laughed this time. "Really?" she asked him, looking down at the small piece of paper in her hands.

"In case you come to your senses," Monty said.

Sharon couldn't believe he had the gall to say such a thing. "Well," she said, "I've never been very sensible," pressed the paper back into his hand, and walked away.

Sharon wondered how long his mouth would be hanging open like that, and she smiled. She was made of stronger stuff than she thought.

1. When you have ended a relationship such as Sharon's, have you felt regret afterwards?

_____

_____

_____

Share more about this question.

_____

_____

_____

_____

_____

_____

_____

_____

Option 2B2:

"That's probably a good idea," Monty said. Sharon heard the edge in his voice. She knew he was upset.

As she buttoned up her blouse, put on her sweater and shoes, Monty pulled on his trousers and slipped on his own shoes. "I'll walk you back," he said. Still with that edge.

"That's not necessary," she said.

"No, it is," he said, and his voice was gentler this time.

The next day, after breakfast, Monty asked if he could speak with Sharon on the deck. As they walked in the morning sunshine, he said, "I'm sorry. I shouldn't have pushed you last night. I was drunk, and I wasn't being respectful."

"Thank you," Sharon said. "I appreciate that. And honestly, you aren't the only one who was drunk."

Monty laughed.

"I don't think either of us were at our best," Sharon said.

"Do you think we can start fresh?" Monty asked.

Sharon nodded and reached out to squeeze his hand.

They agreed to take things slow for the rest of the trip, and continued to enjoy each other's company. On the last day of the cruise, they exchanged phone numbers and made a date for coffee the following week.

As Sharon picked up her suitcase on the dock, she realized Lucy had been right. She did feel better, lighter, and she definitely had something to look forward to.

For Reflection: Summary of your responses to Sharon's story:

Describe a personal situation similar to Sharon's.

1. How did it play out for you? Were you happy with the outcome?

_____

_____

_____

2. After reading this, would you have done it differently?

_____

_____

_____

3. What else would you like to share?

_____

_____

_____

4. Even if you can't relate to this situation, where might you find a point of connection to this story?

_____

_____

_____

5. Have you ever felt like Sharon did at any point in the story?

_____

_____

_____

"*There are more than 110 million sexually transmitted infections among men and women in the United States, and there are 20 million new infections each year, according to the Centers for Disease Control and Prevention.*"

"*Its report includes eight common sexually transmitted infections: chlamydia, gonorrhea, hepatitis B virus, herpes, HIV, HPV, syphilis and trichomoniasis.*"

Alcohol alert from NIAAA

The End

What's Possible: Sally's Story

On the first day of August, sitting on her back steps with her morning coffee, Sally realized she'd been single and just shy of celibate (that one late-night rendezvous with Roy back in March) for nine months now. That's long enough to have produced a baby, Sally thought, and then laughed. At fifty-four, she was a little past procreation.

Honestly, she'd always felt a little past it. Although all of her friends got out of high school, married and dove right into motherhood, Sally's path had been different.

She'd had a few long-term relationships, the longest of which was Roy, with whom she even lived for ten years. But when Roy started to feel more like a roommate than a partner or even a friend, Sally knew it was time to end things. She missed the day-to-day dinner companion, but she hadn't missed the feeling of being lonely with another person in the room, which she'd been reminded of immediately after having sex with Roy the last time. *That* was a mistake.

After that, Sally stuck to the celibacy thing and let herself enjoy platonic time with friends and coworkers, like Mandy. Mandy played on a women's softball team. When the team qualified for an out of town tournament, she invited Sally along for what sounded like a fun mini-vacation a few hours away from home.

Sally had agreed, and they were scheduled to leave town the first day of August. The road trip itself was a hoot - lots of laughter, more coffee, donuts and dirty jokes. For the first time, Sally wasn't the only unmarried woman who'd never been a mother in the group. Even better, everyone on Mandy's team was friendly and seemed to enjoy Sally's company. Sally especially liked Suzanne, who could get the whole group cracking up with just about any story she told.

That night, on the way home, Sally was surprised when Mandy mentioned that Suzanne seemed to really like Sally. Mandy winked.

Although Sally wasn't quite sure what that meant, she didn't want to seem stupid and ask, so she just said, "Oh."

On Sunday morning, while everyone loaded suitcases and duffel bags into the van for the trip home, Suzanne approached Sally.

"Hey," Suzanne said. "I had a lot of fun getting to know you this weekend. Maybe we could exchange numbers?"

1. If Sally got uncomfortable at Suzanne's request, turn to page 45.

2. If Sally was intrigued at the idea of spending more time with Suzanne, turn to page 49.

Option 1:

Sally recognized the look in Suzanne's eyes. Sally had seen it before in men she'd dated, and seeing it in Suzanne made her feel like someone had just pulled the rug right out from under her.

"Why would we do that?" Sally asked, and crossed her arms. She noticed her own voice sound far away.

"Well, maybe so we could call each other," Suzanne said in a deadpan tone and then smiled.

Sally wanted to laugh, but she also wished she could be anywhere else but here. "Not so we would go out or anything, I assume," she heard herself say, in that far-away voice, "because I'm not gay or anything. I haven't had a date in a long time, but I'm not that desperate." Sally also heard herself laugh even though she knew what she'd just said was officially awful.

"Whoa," Suzanne said. That look of attraction in her eyes froze into anger. "There's no need to be like that."

"Like what?" Sally asked, and wished she would just stop talking.

"Although someone like you would never know it, I'm actually a great catch," Suzanne said. "And too bad for you, you're never going to find out."

As Suzanne walked away, Sally had the sinking feeling that this van ride wasn't going to be nearly as enjoyable as the one on the way here.

1. Have you ever found yourself being attracted to another woman?

_____

_____

_____

2. What was that experience like for you?

_____

_____

_____

3. What were the benefits to your knowledge of yourself?

_____

_____

_____

4. What were the unanswered questions you might have had?

_____

_____

_____

Option 2:

Sally recognized the look in Suzanne's eyes. She had seen it before in men she'd dated, and seeing it in Suzanne made her feel like someone had just pulled the rug right out from under her.

"Why would we do that?" Sally asked, curious.

"Well, maybe so we could call each other," Suzanne said in a deadpan tone and then smiled.

Sally laughed. "Yeah, I guess that would be the next logical step."

Since Sally didn't have any paper, Suzanne wrote her number on a napkin from her pocket.

When she handed it to Sally, Sally surprised herself by saying, "Want to come over to watch a movie next Saturday?"

"You know," Suzanne said, "That would be great."

Sally was nervous and excited all day Saturday. She cleaned the whole house, and even found herself singing as she vacuumed. An hour before Suzanne was to arrive, Sally took a shower, put on jeans, and tried on six different shirts before she decided on a simple v-neck T-shirt in her favorite bright yellow.

Sally relaxed as soon as Suzanne arrived, also in jeans and a T-shirt. Suzanne reached into her bulky shoulder bag and pulled out a bottle of merlot and a bar of dark chocolate. "No movie is complete without these," she said.

"I couldn't agree more," Sally said.

During the movie, Suzanne sat close to Sally on the couch. Although they didn't touch, Sally could feel electricity in the few inches between them. She noticed Suzanne's perfume, something a little sweet and a little citrusy. Something delicious.

The movie turned out to be sappier than Sally expected, and she couldn't help but cry at the happy ending.

When Suzanne said, "Pass the Kleenex. It got me, too, damn it," Sally laughed.

Sally turned the TV off and asked if Suzanne needed some more wine or anything.

Suzanne took Sally's hand in hers, raised it to her lips and kissed it. "Nope," she said.

Sally looked at her hand and then into Suzanne's eyes, and soon Sally found herself kissing another woman for the first time.

Suzanne took the bottom of the yellow shirt it had taken Sally so long to choose and slid it up over her head. As Sally lowered her bare arms, goosebumps popped up from her wrists to her shoulders, and she wasn't sure if this was a good or bad sign.

"Hold on," Sally said. "Shouldn't we talk about this?"

"Talk about what?"

"I don't know," Sally said, thinking back on her encounters with men, trying to remember what she was supposed to do at this point. Wondering if what she knew even applied. She swallowed hard. "So, this is new territory for me. I haven't been with a woman before. Do we need some kind of, you know, protection?"

"Lesbians can't get HIV," Suzanne said, "if that's what you're worried about."

"Yes, female to female transmission of HIV is possible, and it has happened. Unfortunately, to date there have not been many studies that have examined lesbian sexual acts and the transmission of HIV."

About.com Guide

---

1. If Sally lets Suzanne keep undressing her, turn to page 53.

2. If Sally says, "That's not true," turn to page 59.

Option 2A

"That's not really what I was worried about," Sally said.

"Then what are you worried about?" Suzanne asked.

"Well," Sally said, "I'm not sure what to do."

"In that case," Suzanne said, smiling, "Relax. I've got you covered."

Sally nodded and let Suzanne take over. The way Suzanne touched her was new. It wasn't gentle exactly, but there was a softness, a grace none of Sally's male partners, especially Roy, had ever had. With men, Sally had always felt small, like the only important part of her was the opening between her legs.

This was different. Suzanne seemed to want all of her. Kissed her everywhere. Although she'd only had one glass of the merlot, Sally felt drunk. She felt soft, like a rag doll. She even let Suzanne take her hand and lead Sally into her bedroom.

Suzanne pulled back the comforter and told Sally to stretch out on the sheets. "I'll be right back," Suzanne said.

Sally knew she was in her own bed, but lying there, waiting for Suzanne, she might as well have been on a different planet.

Suzanne returned with her purse and sat down on the edge of the bed. She grinned at Sally. "I brought some toys," she said. "Interested?"

Sally couldn't help but imagine Suzanne pulling out a bag full of Legos or Play-Doh. She stifled a nervous giggle. "Sure," she made herself say.

When Suzanne pulled out a long, thick, copper colored vibrator, Sally didn't feel like giggling anymore. Her body tensed. Suzanne turned it on and the buzzing noise made Sally think her room was swarming with flies. Not a sexy thought.

Sally felt like she was in one of those dreams where some bad guy is chasing you, when you can't run, can't move. Sally watched as Suzanne ran the vibrator along Sally's thigh and used it to push her legs apart. Part of her was excited, but a bigger part of her was scared. Sally watched the tip of the vibrator moving closer to the center of her, and she couldn't take it anymore. She reached up and pushed Suzanne's hand away. Sally pulled herself back against the headboard, held her knees to her chest.

"Whoa," Suzanne said, eyes wide. "You okay?"

"I just need a minute," Sally said.

"Sure," Suzanne said. "That's fine." Suzanne turned off the vibrator and put it aside. She pulled the comforter up over Sally. "What if I make us some tea?"

Sally nodded, holding the comforter up to her neck. She took some deep breaths and closed her eyes. She was glad to be covered up again.

After ten minutes or so, when Suzanne walked back into the room wearing her T-shirt and underwear, Sally was feeling much calmer, sitting up and able to stretch out her legs again. Now she just felt a little embarrassed, wondering what Suzanne must think of her. Figuring she probably blew it.

Suzanne had two mugs in one hand and Sally's shirt in the other. "Thought you might want this," Suzanne said, handing her the shirt. Suzanne set one of the mugs on Sally's nightstand.

"Thanks," Sally said. She pulled the shirt over her head.

"How are you doing?" Suzanne asked. She didn't look mad. She looked genuinely concerned.

"Better," Sally said.

"Good," Suzanne said, squeezing Sally's hand. "I'm sorry if I freaked you out."

Thankful for Suzanne's kindness, Sally explained that she had been scared, but that she was also enjoying herself. She wondered if they could try again another time, and to Sally's relief, Suzanne agreed.

"Whenever you're ready," Suzanne said.

After they finished their tea, Sally walked Suzanne to the door and hugged her goodbye. The hug was short and sweet, which Sally appreciated. Less possibility for confusion.

"Hey," Suzanne said, "I've wanted to go hear that bluegrass band in Mid-City. Maybe we could do that next Friday night, after work?"

"I've never been," Sally said, "That's a great idea. Let's do it."

1. What did you feel as you read this section?

_____

_____

_____

2. Could this be an experience that you would want to have or absolutely not? Describe in more detail.

_____

_____

_____

3. Do you feel judgmental about the characters in this section? Explain.

_____

_____

_____

Option 2B

"That's not true," Sally said. "Anyone can get HIV."

"Well, not me," Suzanne said, leaning back. "I'm clean. Ladies only. Really, I should be worried about you." Sally realized that Suzanne's wit wasn't the only part of her that could be sharp.

"Hey," Sally said, feeling exposed and vulnerable, sitting across from this woman she realized she barely knew. "I wasn't accusing you of anything. That's not even what I was worried about."

> *"It is worth mentioning that many women who identify as lesbians have had sex with a man at least once in their lives. For various reasons, women who identify as lesbians are less likely to use protection during sexual encounters with men. This increases the risk of disease transmission as the fact that many lesbians' male sexual partners, when they have them, tend to be at higher risk than partners of heterosexual women."*
>
> **Elizabeth Boskey, Pd. D.**
> **(About.com Guide, updated Feb. 3rd, 2013)**

"Then what were you worried about?" Suzanne asked.

"Well," Sally said, "I'm not sure what to do." As soon she said it, she felt like an idiot. An amateur. What did she think she was playing at anyway? Sally reached for her T-shirt, crumpled on the floor next to the couch.

Suzanne grabbed Sally's wrist before she could pick it up. "In that case," Suzanne said, smiling, "relax. I've got you covered."

Suzanne took Sally's face in her hands and kissed her. In that moment, Suzanne officially became the best kisser Sally had ever encountered. Suzanne's kiss was passionate, artful, slow then fast, hard and soft.

"A number of STDs can also be transmitted from woman to woman. A higher number of female partners has been associated with increased risk of bacterial vaginosis, herpes, and HPV in various studies. There is also evidence that lesbian sex can transmit trichomoniasis and hepatitis. This risk is compounded by the fact that many lesbians and bisexual women consider sex between women to be a low-risk activity and so do not practice safer sex."

Elizabeth Boskey, Ph. D.
(About.com Guide, updated Feb 3rd 2013)

Sally struggled to think clearly. Just a minute ago, Suzanne seemed pretty pissed off, and now she was hot to trot. Not that it didn't feel good, not that it wasn't exciting when Suzanne gently whispered, "Mother, may I?" with her hands on the back hook of Sally's bra, letting Sally nod before she unhooked it and slid the straps down over her shoulders.

When Suzanne pushed Sally back on the couch, that was exciting too, but the way Suzanne unbuttoned Sally's jeans, so fast that she even scratched Sally in the process, introduced something else into the equation: fear.

"Suzanne," Sally said, reaching out to stop Suzanne's hands. "I'm feeling a little nervous here."

"Oh, sweet Sally," Suzanne said. "You're nervous?" She kissed each of Sally's hands, one and a time, then put them down next to her. "Well, I know what to do about that, too." Suzanne pressed Sally's hands into the couch, leaned down and started to pull Sally's jeans down with her teeth.

Sally wanted to say, "That's not what I meant," but her cell phone ringing stopped them both. Suzanne lifted her head at the sound, and Sally clutched at the pause in the action to pull her hands away from Suzanne's grasp and jump up from the couch. "I should get that."

In the hallway, Sally re-buttoned her jeans with one hand as she answered her phone with the other. It was Mandy, wondering if they wanted to join her and some of the others from the team for a late dinner at China Kitchen. She was in the neighborhood and could swing by and pick them up in ten.

"That sounds great," Sally said, relieved. Help was on the way. She hadn't been sure how to stop what was happening on her own, but this seemed like a great excuse.

"So," Sally said, walking back into the living room, "that was Mandy. She offered to swing by and pick us up for dinner with her and some of the team."

Suzanne was stretched out on the couch. Her shirt was off now, too, and she said, "And I'm sure you told her you were very busy." Suzanne smirked and patted the cushion next to her.

Sally stopped walking toward the couch and stood where she was. "Actually, I'm kind of starving, so I said yes. Late night Chinese food?"

Suzanne sat bolt upright. "Are you fucking kidding me? We were in the middle of something here. In case you hadn't noticed."

"I know," Sally said. "I just thought we could use a breather."

"Oh, poor little scared Sally needs a breather from the big bad lesbian," Suzanne said, standing. There was that sharp edge again.

"That's not what I said."

"Listen," Suzanne said. "You said you didn't know what to do, and you were about to get a gold medal private lesson. So why don't you just call Mandy back and tell her you're otherwise engaged."

"Because," Sally said, "I don't want to."

"You sure wanted something a minute ago."

"Well maybe that's true, but I'm changing my mind really fast over here," Sally said. "I think you should go."

"You little tease," Suzanne said, her voice low and ugly. "Why don't you call me when you're ready to play with the big kids?"

Sally didn't know what to say. She just wished this evening had never happened and that Mandy might get here early. The transformation in Suzanne left her unsteady. She held herself against the doorway out into the hall.

Without putting on her shirt, Suzanne pulled on her jacket, shoved her shirt into her purse, and yanked it up so quickly that she knocked over both wine glasses. One shattered on the edge of the table. "Better yet," she said, "don't call me at all. You've got too much of a mess here for me to deal with."

Sally leaned hard into the wall as Suzanne stormed by, slamming the door behind her on the way out. Sally locked the door and walked to the living room to pick up her own T-shirt.

With shaky hands, she pulled it over her head. She grimaced thinking how much energy she had put into picking out what to wear and how quickly this first date had plummeted into something she wasn't ready for. If it took her so much effort to figure out what to put on, maybe next time she should put at least the same effort into deciding whether or not to take it off.

1. Have you ever had any kind of sexual experience where anger or physical aggressiveness was exhibited?

_____

_____

_____

2. Was it scary? . . . Or . . . please describe.

_____

_____

_____

3. Was this situation resolved or did it cause the end of the relationship?

_____

_____

_____

4.   How did this incident affect future relation-ships?

_____

_____

_____

The End

Left to Her Own Devices: Beth's Story

To celebrate two years of living clean and sober, Beth decided to go to an NA Conference with Jean, who had been a great friend to Beth these last few years.

The morning of the first day of the conference, Jean called to say her dad had just gone into the hospital. "But you should still go to the conference," Jean added.

"I don't know," Beth said. "Maybe I should come to the hospital to be with you." As weird as it seemed, the hospital actually sounded safer to Beth. She hadn't been out to any big event by herself in a while, and the idea of a big conference was a little intimidating.

"I'll be fine. My brother will be there with me. But support your recovery and go have fun! I'm sure you'll meet great people," Jean said. "And try to learn more about relapse prevention."

Jean had always given Beth good advice, so Beth drove out to the airport conference hotel, parked her car, took a big gulp of air, and walked in by herself.

As Beth took her room keys and registration packet, she noticed a man about her age, standing against the wall between two tall silk plants. He saw her too and smiled, put his arms around the plants like they were his buddies, and she smiled back.

Beth thought about going over and introducing herself, but decided just to wave and head to the first presentation instead. Still painfully aware of relationship choices she'd made as an addict, Beth hadn't spoken to a lot of men since she got clean. She wished Jean was here. Beth needed a wing woman.

Despite her efforts to keep focused on the conference, the "plant man" seemed to be in every meeting she attended, including the last one of the day, during which she'd drummed up the courage to share her story out loud, including the parts about domestic violence and criminal behavior.

Beth wasn't surprised when he approached her after the session.

"Where are your plant friends?" Beth asked, still feeling the adrenaline from talking in front of fifty people.

"I decided to fly solo," he said. "Karl."

"Beth."

Karl told her that she was really brave to talk so candidly about the hard lessons she'd learned and her journey to recovery.

He got her a cup of tea and they sat in the last row of the red velvet hotel conference chairs.

They spent a long time talking, and Karl was a good listener. Beth liked that he wasn't one of those guys who didn't let her get a word in edgewise. He actually asked questions. She did, too, and they traded stories. Some made them laugh, but others, not so much. At one point, the memory of an ugly fight with Beth's ex felt so vivid that she started to cry.

Karl put his arm around her, and Beth rested her head on his shoulder. It felt good to be held.

When a guy from the cleaning crew said they needed to lock up the room, Karl suggested they go offsite for a bite to eat later and offered to walk Beth her back to her room in the meantime.

1. If Beth agrees to meet up with Karl later, turn to page 71.

2. If Karl asks to come into her room and she agrees, turn to page 83.

Option 1:

After such a good conversation, Beth didn't think it would hurt to go grab a late night snack with Karl. She wasn't all that excited about hotel food anyway.

When he dropped her off at her room, they agreed to meet in the lobby at eight.

"Is it okay to give you a hug?" Karl asked.

"Sure," Beth said, liking that he asked first. The hug was nice, even if it lasted a little longer than Beth felt comfortable with.

They took a cab to a fun part of town - a stretch of cafés, bars and shops - and decided on a diner for some breakfast comfort food. Beth was feeling a little weird about the hug from earlier, but their dinner conversation was fun and lighthearted and Beth relaxed a little.

Midway through pancakes, Karl got a text and said, "Want to go to a party with me? A good friend of mine is having it - he's a nice guy. It should be clean," he added quickly.

"*At this time, the principal risk for acquiring hepatitis C appears to be the use of injection drugs, primarily IV drug abuse. IV drug users comprise upwards of 40% of those who are diagnosed with new cases of hepatitis C. Other high-risk activities include other drug use (including intra-nasal cocaine use). People with multiple sex partners are also considered to be at high risk (although the actual risk of sexual transfer of this disease is thought to be relatively low).*"

MEDICINENET.com

Beth said, "Let me think about it while I visit the ladies room." In the bathroom, Beth called Jean, but just got voicemail.

Beth thought, I can do this. It's not like I'm a kid. I'm a grown woman. It's okay to have a life and go to a party with a nice guy.

She checked in the mirror for any stray food stuck in her teeth. All clear.

Karl's friend Randy's house was nice, and so was Randy. Although Beth really wanted the glass of wine Randy offered, she felt good declining it and accepting some iced tea instead.

This was turning out to be a really fun night. Until a tall thin guy sat between Karl and Beth on the couch, put his arms around them both and said, "Who wants to party? We're heading to the basement."

"Beth, meet Vince. Old college buddy. Vince, Beth, my new friend."

"Well new friend Beth," Vince said, squeezing her shoulder, "want to party?"

1. If Beth decides to leave, turn to page 75 1A.

2. If Beth decides to stay, turn to page 79 1B.

Option 1A:

Beth peeled Vince's arm off of her shoulder and stood up. "And that's our cue to leave," Beth said, proud of how confident she sounded.

But Karl wasn't getting up.

"Or at least it's my cue," she said. "Are you coming?"

"We just got here," Karl said.

"That's right," Vince said. "It's too early to leave. And you can't take the life of the party with you." Vince punched Karl on the arm.

"Well, he's welcome to stay if he wants," Beth said, "I'm calling a cab."

Back in her hotel room, after a shower, a big glass of water, and a bag of M&Ms, Beth was just crawling under the covers when Jean called.

"Hey," Jean said. "Got your message. Everything okay?"

"Just fine," Beth said. "Everything's just fine."

1. Summarize your past sexual behavior while in your active addiction.

_____

_____

_____

2. How has sobriety/recovery affected you sexual behavior?

_____

_____

_____

3. What are still triggers for you around sexual behavior?

_____

_____

_____

4. Does this story support more options for those triggers?

_____

_____

_____

Option 1B:

Beth peeled Vince's arm off of her shoulder and scooted a few inches over on the couch. "And that's probably our cue to leave," Beth said, looking to Karl for confirmation.

But Karl wasn't getting up. "We did just get here," Karl said.

"That's right," Vince said. "It's too early to leave. And you can't take the life of the party with you." Vince punched Karl on the arm.

Karl laughed, and Beth liked the sound of his laugh. She felt the tingle of possibility, the sense that something exciting could happen.

"We can keep an eye on each other," Karl said to Beth. He turned to Vince, "Beth and I don't party like you party anymore."

"That's cool," Vince said. "You could at least hang out, right? Check out the sweet stuff I brought and decide later if you want it?"

"That sounds reasonable," Karl said. "Beth?"

Maybe Beth could just have her iced tea and some good laughs while everyone else did whatever they wanted to do in the basement. Or maybe just half a glass of wine.

Vince stood up and said, "Who's coming?"

Karl stood up and held out his hand to help Beth up. They followed Vince into the basement, which seemed darker and louder than Randy's bright living room.

Beth struggled to even see the steps, and she lost her footing a few times on the way down.

1. Summarize your past sexual behavior while in your active addiction.

_____

_____

_____

2. How has sobriety/recovery affected your sexual behavior?

_____

_____

_____

3. What are still triggers for you around sexual behavior?

_____

_____

_____

4. Does this story offer more options for dealing with triggers?

_____

_____

_____

Option 2:

"I don't know about later tonight," Beth said. That sounded dangerous. "But you're welcome to walk me upstairs."

At the door to her room, Karl asked if he could give her a hug.

"Sure," Beth said, liking that he asked.

The hug lasted a little longer than a friendly hug does, and Beth felt herself wanting more. They separated slowly and soon the hug turned into a kiss.

"Maybe we should go inside?" Karl whispered into her ear.

Beth nodded and fumbled to open the door with the key card.

Inside, Beth's heart was hammering against her chest. She was more nervous than she'd been talking in front of all of those people. The taste of Karl's lips made her suddenly, desperately want the taste of wine.

1. If Karl gets pushy and aggressive, turn to page 85 2A.

2. If Karl notices she's uncomfortable and asks her what's up, turn to page 89 2B.

Option 2A:

Karl grabbed Beth by the shoulders and kissed her, harder than their hallway kiss. Beth was finding it hard to think.

She pulled back.

"Hey," Karl said, "I'm not done with those lips." He grabbed her again and pulled her tight against him, pressed his lips against hers.

This wasn't fun anymore.

With some effort, Beth pulled away again and grabbed the doorknob just as Karl grabbed her other wrist.

She forced open the door and used all of her strength to pull herself out into the hallway. "You should go," she said.

"Fine," Karl said, smiling through gritted teeth at the couple - one tall woman, one short - walking past Beth's room toward the elevator. The two women turned back around and watched until Karl said, "I'll see you around," and strode past them to the stairs.

"Thanks," Beth said to the couple.

"You're welcome," the taller woman said. Her smile was like her friend Jean's. "We've got to look out for each other. You okay?"

"Yes," Beth said, rubbing her wrist where Karl had grabbed it. "I'll be fine."

1. Have you ever been involved in a physically abusive situation?

_____

_____

_____

2. Was the outcome what you had hoped for?

_____

_____

_____

3. How has that affected your relationships since then?

_____

_____

_____

4. Did these incidents cause a relapse? If not, what was your choice of action that prevented this?

_____

_____

_____

Option 2B:

Beth's hands were shaking so badly that the key dropped to the ground.

Karl picked it up and handed it to her. "Hey," he said, "are you okay?"

"Sure," Beth said. "Just a little nervous."

"That was really fun right there in the hallway," Karl said, "but I think it's time for me to go."

Beth resisted the urge to beg him to stay, to go grab a box of wine and hole up with him in the hotel room for the rest of the conference. She nodded, but noticed tightness in her jaw.

"I feel like it would be a good idea for me to find a meeting to go to later. If you want to come with me, I'm in room 301." He touched her arm lightly.

"Thanks," Beth said. "That seems like a really good idea."

1. If you are in a relationship now, does your partner respect and support your recovery?

_____

_____

_____

2. If you could ask something of your partner to support your recovery, what would that be?

_____

_____

_____

3. Have you noticed that this relationship is taking time away from recovery activities?

_____

_____

_____

The End

How Fast Should We Go? Ann's Story

To celebrate her twenty-fifth year of running Human Resources for Vita-Tech, the office staff threw Ann a party.

On the outside, she smiled through the whole thing, saying thank you, eating cake, drinking punch with a little champagne. On the inside, Ann felt hollow.

I'm sixty-four years old, and this is the anniversary I get?

Ann had never married or even had a long-term boyfriend. Focusing on her career instead of getting married and having a family had always seemed like a good choice. She'd had plenty of one-night stands, and had always prided herself on being able just to enjoy the sex without expectations of a relationship. And she'd had plenty of sex over the years - some protected, some not - but all lots of fun.

Still, that night after the party, curled up in her robe on the couch with her cat, Ann felt lonely.

When her best friend Louise called and asked about the party, Ann burst into tears.

After Louise coaxed the story out of her, she said, "Honey, it's time. I'm going to come over and help you do your profile this weekend."

Louise had been recommending the dating service she'd used to meet her boyfriend Daryl. This time, Ann said, "Okay, no backing out now."

At first, Ann wrote short answers on her application, but as she got into the process, she found herself typing faster, adding more information, enjoying articulating what she wanted, what she desired. She included recent pictures of herself from the Glamour Shots she and Louise had taken on a whim.

By Monday morning, Ann's inbox overflowed with responses to her profile. Delighted and a little over-whelmed, she decided to start small and contact the two men, Jeff and Bill, who seemed most interesting to her.

By lunchtime, Bill wrote her back, saying it was great to hear from her and that he thought she was so beautiful in her picture that she must be a knockout in person. He might need a team of paramedics on hand.

Although it was a little over the top, it was nice to receive a compliment. Ann wrote back to say thank you and to say that she liked the picture of him fishing at the lake.

And then he wrote back again.

That was the most exciting afternoon Ann had had at work in years. Writing back and forth with Bill made her feel like she was in high school. Little sugary notes, passed electronically. Maybe not serious nutrition, but it was fun.

In between tasks, she checked her messages, and by five o'clock, as she was closing up her email, Bill asked if she wanted to meet for dinner and drinks that weekend. It seemed fast, but she remembered how lonely she'd been last weekend and wrote back a quick "Yes."

The next morning at work, Ann had a message from Jeff. His message was more demure, and he asked lots of great questions, wondering, for instance what was the best book she'd read recently and why she loved it.

Ann responded right away with questions of her own, but by the end of the day, she still hadn't heard back from Jeff. A little disappointing. In the meantime, she had made dinner plans with Bill for Friday. And Bill kept her completely distracted with little flirty notes throughout the day.

By Wednesday, Ann had received a nice long response from Jeff. She read the email three times in a row, savoring his thoughtfulness and intelligence. She was wishing her Friday night date was with Jeff instead and wondered if she should just ask him out for Saturday.

1. If Ann asks Jeff to go out on Saturday evening, turn to page 95.

2. If Ann decides to just keep corresponding with Jeff, turn to page 101.

Option 1:

Bill asked me out the first day we wrote to each other, so what the heck? Why not ask Jeff? Two dates in one weekend could be really exciting.

Ann wrote back to Jeff and did her best to sound playful and flirty and fun, asking if he'd be up for drinks and some dancing on Saturday. She was nervous when she hit send, but did it anyway.

Ann didn't hear from Jeff for the rest of the week, but by Friday, all she could think about what getting ready for her date with Bill.

Louise came over to help her pick out an outfit, a sapphire dress she hadn't worn in five years. Ann had forgotten how much she loved that dress, how the skirt swirled when she walked. Louise said it brought out the green in her eyes.

Bill did, too, when she walked into the restaurant. He even kissed her hand. Ann had worried she might not be attracted to him in person, but the chemistry was instantaneous.

> *"Alcohol use is associated with high-risk sexual behaviors and injection drug use, two major modes of HIV transmission."*
>
> ### Alcohol and HIV/AIDS / Alcohol Alert
> ### from the NIAAA

Dinner melted into drinks at a swanky jazz bar, and before Ann knew it, they were back at her house and naked, on her couch. The sex was great - passionate, raw, not a lot of talking, just how Ann liked it.

The next morning, she noticed a few drops of blood on the couch. As she cleaned them off, she figured they must have been from running her nails down Bill's back. She got flushed thinking about how aggressive they had both been. It was a wild night for sure.

When Bill got up, they had coffee and Ann made a big omelet they could share.

She could get used to this - shared breakfast, intimate affection, someone to do the crossword with.

After breakfast, Bill kissed her on the lips and said, "I'll call you."

Ann felt a little funny hearing those words, but chose to ignore them and dream about future evenings and mornings with Bill. She even took herself shopping on Sunday to get a new dress to wear for their next date.

By Monday morning, Bill still hadn't called, and Ann knew why she had felt a little funny on Saturday. He wasn't going to call. It was just a one-night thing. She knew one when she saw one, but just wasn't being honest with herself about it.

At work, Ann was excited to see a message from Jeff, thinking her day might turn around. She quickly forgot about the bad start of her morning. Jeff had even sent the message on Friday night, while she was out with Bill. Jeff wrote that although he'd enjoyed their initial emails, he had to decline her offer to go out. Jeff said he'd learned that anytime someone made a date so fast, it just wasn't a good match for him. He preferred to get to know someone.

Ann felt discouraged, not sure she was cut out for this online dating thing or this dating thing at all. Maybe she'd close down her profile.

1. What has been your experience with one night stands?

_____

_____

_____

2. What have you learned?

_____

_____

_____

3. What are you trying to do differently?

_____

_____

_____

4. Do you have a friend whom you can role play difficult conversations with in order to be your honest self?

_____

_____

_____

Option 2:

No, Ann decided, these messages were so nice and luxurious with Jeff. She didn't want to ruin them by rushing things. In fact, there was no reason to write back right now. She'd save it for tomorrow. One date for the weekend was plenty for now.

Ann wrote Jeff back on Thursday, not worrying about when he'd respond. By Friday, all she could think about what getting ready for her date with Bill.

Louise came over to help her pick out an outfit, a sapphire dress she hadn't worn in five years. Ann had forgotten how much she loved that dress, how the skirt swirled when she walked. Louise said it brought out the green in her eyes.

Bill did, too, when she walked into the restaurant. He even kissed her hand. Ann had worried she might not be attracted to him in person, but the chemistry was instantaneous.

Dinner was followed by drinks at a swanky jazz bar, and before she knew it, they were back at her house and naked, on her couch. The sex was great - passionate, raw, not a lot of talking, just how Ann liked it.

The next morning, she noticed a few drops of blood on the couch. As she cleaned them off, she figured they must have been from running her nails down Bill's back.

She got flushed thinking about how aggressive they had both been. It was a wild night for sure.

When Bill got up, they had coffee and Ann made a big omelet they could share. She could get used to this - shared breakfast, intimate affection, someone to do the crossword with.

After breakfast, Bill kissed her on the lips and said, "I'll call you."

Ann felt a little funny hearing those words, but chose to ignore them and dream about future mornings and evenings with Bill. She even took herself shopping on Sunday to get a new dress to wear for their next date.

By Monday, Bill still hadn't called, and Ann knew why she'd felt a little funny on Saturday morning. He wasn't going to call. It was just a one-night thing. She knew one when she saw one, but just wasn't being honest with herself about it.

At work, Ann was excited to see a message from Jeff. Long and thoughtful, just like the last one. Maybe it was better to take your time.

Ann and Jeff wrote back and forth for the next several weeks. She noticed that he'd mentioned his love for hot chocolate a few times, and she knew a café that made the best European style chocolate in town. She asked how he would feel about getting together for a morning chocolate date. He said that would be lovely.

Over rich and spicy hot chocolate, Ann found herself just as attracted to Jeff as she had been to Bill, although in a different way. She felt like she knew some important things about him. How he valued reading and philosophical discussions, knew how to fix small appliances, loved The Beatles. And that made this date not just different, but special. He wasn't flirty like Bill, but she was able to relax and really enjoy his company.

After two hours and a shared croissant, Jeff said, "I need to go soon. I volunteered to help my friend clean out his garage. But I'd like to see you again."

Ann smiled, relieved. She was hoping he felt the same. "I'd like that."

"And I have to say, you're a beautiful woman, and I'd be interested in pursuing this relationship."

Ann found his honesty and phrasing charming. "I feel the same way," she said.

"Great," Jeff said and went on to explain that it was really important to him that they both be tested for HIV to make sure they were safe. He said he'd been tested a month ago, it was negative, and that he hadn't had a partner since then. He asked if she'd been tested recently and if not, if she would be willing to for the relationship to go forward. He did not, however, ask about her recent relationships, and she didn't offer any information.

Ann felt a little weird about this turn of conversation. She felt small and a little scared, which was ridiculous for a woman like her. She was vice-president of HR for God's sake.

Was this man judging her? Ann thought about her night a few weeks ago with Bill. They hadn't used protection. And a year ago, there'd been that other man, and they hadn't either. She didn't really think this was a problem for her generation, or her sexual orientation. Also, talking about HIV didn't exactly get her turned on and ready to go. "No one's ever asked me that before on a date," Ann said, sitting back in her chair. She didn't feel so close to Jeff anymore.

"Sorry, I didn't mean it to be abrupt", Jeff said. "It's just really important to me."

"Having untreated sexually transmitted infections (STIs) makes it more likely for a person to get HIV. This is especially true for women. Small cuts on the skin of the vagina are hard to notice but may allow HIV to pass into a woman's body."

(US Dept of Health and Human Services)

---

1. If Ann decides to have an HIV test, turn to page 105 2A.

2. If Ann decides not to have an HIV test, turn to page 111 2B.

Option 2A:

Ann realized how defensively she was sitting. It's not like Jeff was making some awful demand of her. He'd actually been respectful and polite.

"No, I'm sorry," Ann said. "You just caught me off guard."

"No problem," Jeff said. "I'm only asking because I'm really interested in you. You're a woman worth getting to know."

Ann smiled. That was a nice compliment to get, and was delivered in a genuine tone. He was a man worth getting to know, too. "I haven't had a recent test," she said, "but I can get one."

Ann called Louise that night and told her about Jeff's request. Louise said, "You know, I've been wondering if I should get one myself. Want to go together?"

The next afternoon, Ann and Louise headed to the women's clinic for their tests. Ann felt self-conscious signing in, wondering what people would think if they saw her here.

In the pre-test counseling, the med tech, a woman who seemed to be about Ann's age, asked Ann about her risk factors.

Though she felt embarrassed, Ann was honest and shared about her date with Bill. Thinking it might get a smile out of the med tech, Ann decided to add that she'd found drops of blood on her couch afterward. A shared naughty secret always seemed to break the ice.

Instead, the med tech said, "Ann, I strongly encourage you to be tested for syphilis, gonorrhea and other sexually transmitted infections," and didn't change her recommendation even after Ann said she wasn't aware of any symptoms.

After the counseling and tests, Ann was exhausted. She met Louise back out in the waiting room and Louise said, "That was brave of us. This calls for ice cream."

Ann didn't feel brave; she felt nervous about the results. On the bright side, she did feel like she'd been responsible about sex for the first time in her life. This relationship, if she could call it that, with Jeff, was something brand new, something that filled her with hope.

When Ann and Louise went back a week later for their results, Ann found herself holding her breath in the waiting room.

"You okay?" Louise asked.

"Just thinking about work," Ann lied. "I've got a tough meeting ahead this week."

During her appointment, the med-tech told Ann that her HIV status was negative but that she needed to come back in three months for a re-test. Ann was puzzled, but the med tech reported that the tests had also revealed Chlamydia and herpes.

Ann's heart sank. In addition to the re-test, the tech suggested treatment as well as that Ann contact her partner so he could also be treated.

Ann's head felt crowded with all of the information: what caused Chlamydia, how you could get re-infected, the long-term issues of herpes, the need to use condoms and certainly a dental dam when she was receiving oral sex for the rest of her life.

Feeling numb, Ann refused further counseling but agreed to receive treatment and then come back to be tested.

When she came out of the exam room, Louise took one look at Ann's face and said, "Okay, ready to go?"

They walked quietly out to the car, where Ann burst into tears. She couldn't hold any of it in - the tears, the story about Bill, the results of her test, her fears that Jeff would go running in the other direction when he found out.

"Ann," Louise said, "you're a strong woman. And I really believe this will all work out."

Ann wasn't sure Louise was right, but she appreciated the kindness.

Back at home, Ann was so angry at Bill that she considered not telling him about the STIs. She didn't ever want to talk with him again, for any reason.

But then she thought of other women like her, who might be at risk if she didn't tell him, and that felt worse. Ann dug Bill's phone number out of her email, and was beyond grateful when he didn't answer. Relieved not to have to actually talk with him, she left the information in a voicemail.

As soon as she hung up, the phone rang. God, is he actually calling back?

When she saw Jeff's name on her phone, at first she was just glad it wasn't Bill, but then she remembered she had another tough conversation she wasn't going to be able to avoid.

Ann asked Jeff if they could meet for coffee the next day. When they met, Ann slowly pulled out her negative HIV results, but couldn't look Jeff in the face.

"What's wrong?" Jeff asked.

Ann decided that if she was going to have any chance with this man, she had to be totally honest. She explained that though her HIV test was negative, she had Chlamydia and herpes that she had been unaware of but was now being treated for. She left it at that, and waited, sure he would be disgusted and out the door faster than she could blink.

But Jeff wasn't moving. In a calm voice, he said, "Well, maybe we just need to move more slowly until your treatment is done."

His kindness broke through all of the tension she'd been feeling, and Ann felt the tears coming. She hadn't cried this much in one week since high school

"You know," Jeff said, gently touching her face, "there are a lot of things we can do between now and then."

Ann smiled and realized how lucky she was to have this man in her life. Not only had he encouraged her to do something smart and responsible, but the results of the tests didn't seem to have changed his feelings about her.

She felt like Louise might be right. This really could all work out. Nice and slow, for once. This seemed like exactly the right speed.

1. How important for you is it to be friends with someone before you are intimate?

_____

_____

_____

2. How would you feel about the above scenario being your scenario and what actions would you take?

_____

_____

_____

3. Would you ever initiate this discussion if your partner did not?

_____

_____

_____

Option 2B:

Ann felt like Jeff could see right through her - could see the night with Bill replaying in her mind, could see all of the other nights she'd had. And she felt ashamed.

"I'm sorry," she said, standing up, "I need to go. I don't really want tests to be part of my dating." She thought how silly that sounded, but she couldn't take it back.

"I'm sorry to hear that," Jeff said.

Ann half hoped Jeff might send her a message apologizing, saying he didn't need some silly test that didn't even apply to them to be with her, but she didn't hear from him again.

Ann had a niggling feeling she might be missing something, but forced herself to go back online and move on. She emailed two more men and hoped for the best.

1. Have you ever found yourself in this position?

_____

_____

_____

2. Take some time and write down your list of what is essential for you in a relationship, negotiable for you in a relationship and definitely not negotiable for you in a relationship.

_____

_____

_____

_____

_____

_____

_____

_____

_____

_____

_____

_____

_____

_____

_____

_____

_____

_____

_____

The End

Your Personal Notes . . .

Your Personal Notes . . .

_____

_____

_____

_____

_____

_____

_____

_____

_____

_____

_____

_____

_____

_____

_____

_____

_____

_____

_____

_____

_____

_____

_____

_____

_____

_____

_____

_____

_____

_____

_____

Your Personal Notes . . .

_____

_____

_____

_____

_____

_____

_____

_____

_____

_____

_____

_____

_____

_____

_____

_____

_____

_____

_____

_____

_____

_____

_____

_____

_____

_____

_____

_____

_____

_____

_____

_____

Your Personal Notes . . .

_____

_____

_____

_____

_____

_____

_____

_____

_____

_____

_____

_____

_____

_____

_____

Resources

These resources are forever changing and updating. If you do not have a personal computer to look up this information, libraries and senior centers usually have computers you can use for free. Most now also have free classes for seniors. There are many benefits to "challenging" yourself with new skills and who knows you might even make some new friends. BONUS!

About.com Senior Health: Check out this About.com topic for loads of articles designed to help older people stay healthy and happy.
www.seniorhealth.about.comNIH Senior Health

CDC on Aging: The Centers for Disease Control can be a great place to find information on keeping yourself disease free, prevention screenings and information about specific illnesses.
www.cdc.gov/aging

MedLine Plus Seniors' Health: This site is full of the latest news topics on senior health issues as well as reference materials, prevention and screening resources and much more.
www.nlm.nih.gov/medlineplus/seniorshealth.html

National Institutes of Health: provide seniors with a range of information on topics like bone health, nutrition, exercise and more on this site. Best of all, you can adjust text size or have it read out loud to you.
www.nihseniorhealth.gov

USA.gov for Seniors: Whether you're looking for government links to health resources, volunteering opportunities or even just on retirement you'll find them here.
www/usa.gov/Topics/Seniors.shtml

Other Valuable Sites

www.AA.org – Alcoholic Anonymous, information and support.

www.ACRIA.org - AIDS Community Research Initiative of America.

www.BlackAIDS.org - African American HIV/AIDS Organization.

www.hepcnetwork.org – Caring Ambassadors Program has valuable information about hepatitis C and the challenges people face.

www.HIVAIDSTribe.com - Native American focus.

www.Poz.com - Serves the community of people living with and those affected by HIV/AIDS (broad focus of all ages and cultures).

www.TheAidsInstitute.org - General to specific HIV/AIDS resource.

www.NMAC.org - National Minority AIDS Coalition.

www.NA.org – Narcotics Anonymous support and information.

www.nncam.nih.gov - Complementary medicine information.

www.sisterlove.org - A reproductive justice organization with a focus on HIV/AIDS.

www.thebody.com - For individuals and professionals general to specific information.

www.KFF.org - Kaiser Family Foundation.

Articles and Blogs

Articles and blogs can be found on your internet search and will bring up other options for articles.

Arthritis and Sex: Find out how arthritis may affect your ability to have sex in this short article.

How to Remain Positive About Sex as a Senior: How provides this article for seniors who are struggling with sex as they age who want to take a more optimistic outlook on this.

Merck Manual: Sexuality: Learn how aging, mental illness, and more can affect and change your sexual experience in this guide from Merck.

Midlife Sexuality: InteliHealth provides this article to help those who've lost sexual desire in midlife regain their sexuality.

Nine Health Issues That Can Impact Sexual Satisfaction: If you're having trouble enjoying sex, check out these 9 factors to see if they may be having an impact on your sexual enjoyment.

Seniors and Lifelong Sexual Health: This article explains how sex is an important part of life, even into old age.

Senior Sex: Tips for Older Men: Many men find that as they age they lose the desire or the ability to engage in sex. This article from MSN can help you learn what to do about it.

Sex After 50: Dr. Janice Swanson from the Mayo Clinic offers some advice on how you can keep your sex life healthy and active after 50.

Sexual Health in the Golden Years: Get tips and advice on enjoying sex well into old age by reading this article.

Sexy Seniors: Get ideas on spicing up your sex life, dealing with STDs and more in this blog.

Suddenly Senior's Take On Senior Sex: Find loads of articles related to sex in your older years on this humorous but informative site.

STDs and AIDS in Senior Citizens: STDs are on the rise in senior citizens. Learn to prevent these diseases and reduce your risk in this article.

CPSIA information can be obtained at www.ICGtesting.com
Printed in the USA
BVOW08s2024050813

327913BV00005B/12/P